Merciful Child 3

One day, our prophet
was leading the worship in the mosque.
At that moment, he heard the cry of a child.
Since the child's mother could be worshiping,
he made quick to complete the worship.
He didn't want the child's mother to be disturbed.
By doing that, the mother could hold the child,
and the child would not cry.
Oh our prophet full of mercy and compassion,
we greet you...
Allahumma Salli Ala Sayyidina Muhammed.

Come on let's walk together.
Let's turn the pages.
Why should we be merciful?
Let us color and learn.

Published by:
Erkam Publications
Ikitelli Organize Sanayi Bölgesi
Turgut Özal Cd. No: 117/4
Başakşehir, Istanbul, Turkey
Tel: (90-212) 671-0700 pbx
Fax: (90-212) 671-0717
E-mail: info@islamicpublishing.net
Web site: http://islamicpublishing.net

The author:
Yusuf UNAL

Translator:
Bulent BELBEZ

Redactor:
A. CANDAN

Copy Editor:
Nejla T. ILHAN

Cover Design:
Ali Kaya (Wordgraphics)

Graphics:
Ali KAYA (Wordgraphics)

Dear Mothers and Fathers,

Our children are the greatest treasure entrusted to us.

Our dream is to see that our children have the most beautiful manners.

The "Rose House Coloring Book Series" has focused on the behavior of our children and aimed to gain discipline in them.

This method of teaching these behaviors to preschool children by using coloring and activities is fun and efficient.

In order to use this set efficiently, we should follow the instructions. Parents should guide their children. Every page should be examined carefully.

According to the behaviors mentioned in these pages, parents should exchange ideas with their child.

If we focus on these issues throughout each day, we can encourage display of the desired behaviors.

We recommend that parents color the books with their child in order and one by one. Let us color, think, and apply...

Translated by Bulent Belbez

It was very hot. The dog was thirsty.
The woman passing by could not find a bowl,
so she gave water to the dog with her shoe.

What happens if you don't drink any water all day long?
How would you give water to a thirsty cat?
What would you do if you see a bird with a broken leg?

Elif and Ali were looking at the river water and nearby flowers.
What a beautiful world Allah created for us.
Allah is not born and does not give birth.
He is the Most Merciful.

Which animals live in a river?
Which animals live on land?
Who is the Most Merciful?

Our prophet said,"A two-person meal is enough for three:
a three person meal is enough for four."

Have you ever shared your meal?
What are the children above doing?
Can you tell us?

We should give when our friends ask for something.
We should share our toys with them.
We should smile when we share with them.

Which picture is better in your opinion?
Which child would you prefer to be?
What are the differences between the two pictures?
Can you see the happiness in the faces of the smiling children?

Ali's father bought Ali new clothes.
Ali shared these clothes with the poor children.

Do you give your clothes to anyone?
When does your father buy you clothes?

Ali was on a boat and eating simit (a Turkish pretzel).
He was happier when he shared his simit.

Have you ever been on a boat?
Have you ever thrown feed to the birds?
Can you color after counting the birds?

The lady sitting in the park splits the simit (pretzel). Our prophet said, "Even if you have one date in your hand, share it with the person next to you."

How do you feel if a friend next to you eats something when you are very hungry? What do you share with your friend?

Penguins live at the poles.
In order to protect the egg until the baby comes out,
the father penguin carries the egg on his feet.

Where did the penguin learn this?
Do you know which animals come out of eggs?

Allah gave the feeling of mercy to all living creatures.
The pelican feeds her young with her own mouth.

Who was feeding you when you were a baby?
How do we need to treat our mother?

Our prophet said, "When a person helps his/her brother or sister, Allah helps him or her as well."
Ali's friend wants to help him to carry the bags.

What do you think there are in these bags?
Have you ever helped someone carrying bags?

We should love older people very much.
We should visit the people living in the Rest Home.

Have you ever been in a Rest Home?
How should we treat the older people?
Where do you want your grandmother and grandfather to live?

Ali and Elif remove the rocks on the road that can harm people.

How do you think a rock on the road can harm people?
Has anything on the road given you harm?

Ali's friend was ill. Ali went to visit him.
He brought flowers with him for the visit.

Have you ever visited a friend when he or she was ill?
What would you like to bring when you visit an ill friend?

ACTIVITY PAGE

- The art of folding paper (origami)

Follow the steps:

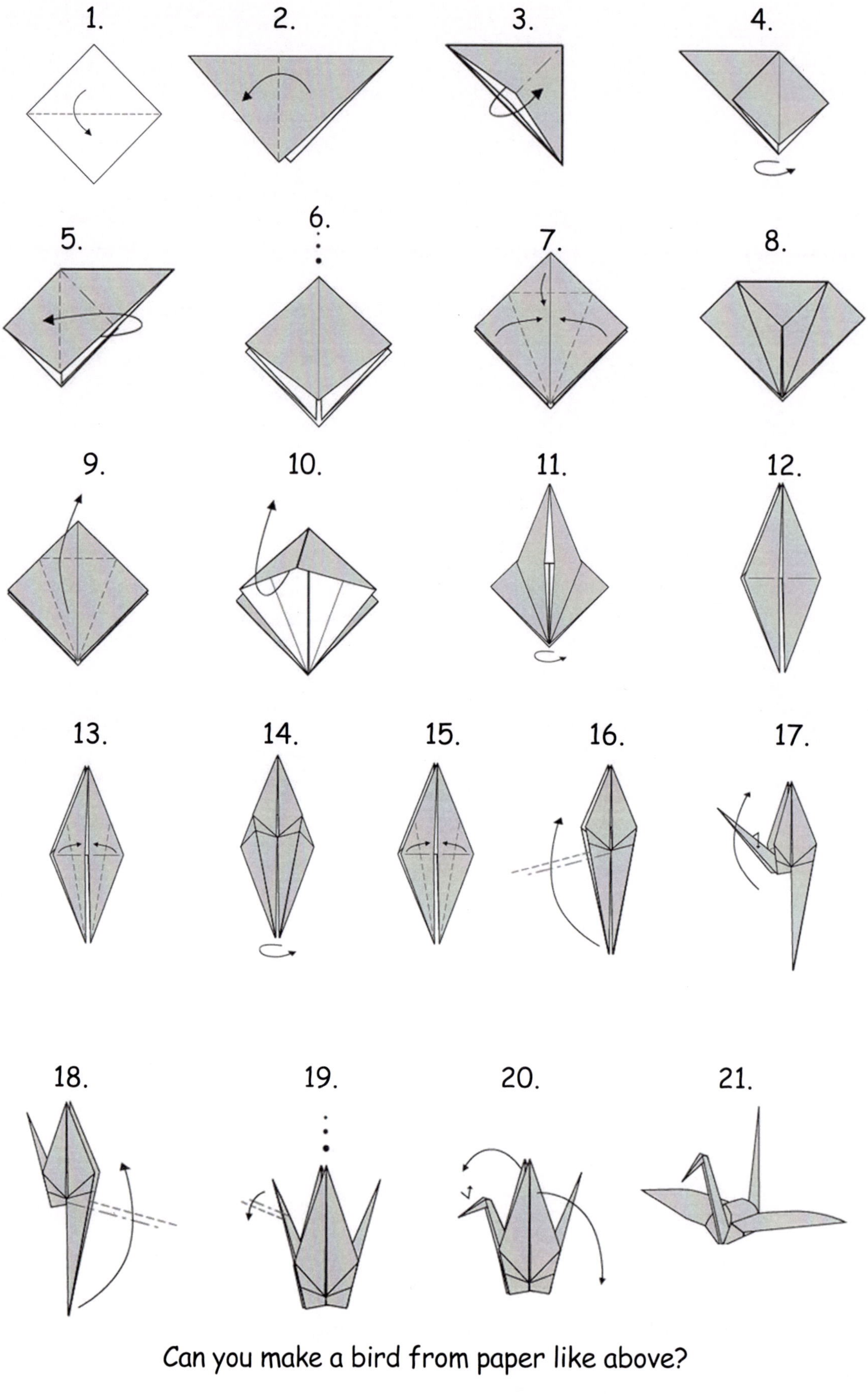

Can you make a bird from paper like above?

9 789366 088976

Printed at Repro India Ltd.